12 REASONS TO LOVE
LACROSSE

by Todd Kortemeier

STORY
LIBRARY

www.12StoryLibrary.com

12-Story Library is an imprint of Bookstaves and Press Room Editions

Produced for 12-Story Library by Red Line Editorial

Photographs ©: Christopher Szagola/Cal Sport Media/AP Images, cover, 1; North Wind Picture Archives, 4; Catwalk Photos/Shutterstock Images, 5, 21; Al Milligan/Icon Sportswire, 6, 28; Vladimir Korostyshevskiy/Shutterstock Images, 7; Brian McEntire/Shutterstock Images, 8, 26; KPG_Payless/ Shutterstock Images, 9; Daniel Kucin Jr./Icon Sportswire/AP Images, 10–11; Larry MacDougal/AP Images, 11, 13; Andrew Vaughan/Canadian Press/AP Images, 12; Gail Burton/AP Images, 15; Library of Congress, 16; Ben Liebenberg/NFL Photos/AP Images, 17; Image Source/Thinkstock, 18; Christopher Szagola/Cal Sport Media/AP Images, 19; Aspen Photo/Shutterstock Images, 20, 29; Mike Broglio/ Shutterstock Images, 22; James A. Boardman/Shutterstock Images, 23; Brocreative/Shutterstock Images, 24; DAJ/Thinkstock, 25; s_bukley/Shutterstock Images, 27

Library of Congress Cataloging-in-Publication Data
Names: Kortemeier, Todd, 1986- author.
Title: 12 reasons to love lacrosse / by Todd Kortemeier.
Other titles: Twelve reasons to love lacrosse
Description: Mankato, MN : 12 Story Library, 2018. | Series: Sports reports |
    Includes bibliographical references and index. | Audience: Grade 4 to 6.
Identifiers: LCCN 2016047093 (print) | LCCN 2016052596 (ebook) | ISBN
    9781632354297 (hardcover : alk. paper) | ISBN 9781632354983 (pbk. : alk.
    paper) | ISBN 9781621435501 (hosted e-book)
Subjects: LCSH: Lacrosse--Juvenile literature.
Classification: LCC GV989.14 .K67 2018 (print) | LCC GV989.14 (ebook) | DDC
    796.36/2--dc23
LC record available at https://lccn.loc.gov/2016047093

Printed in China
022017

Access free, up-to-date content on this topic plus a full digital version of this book. Scan the QR code on page 31 or use your school's login at 12StoryLibrary.com.

Table of Contents

Lacrosse Evolved from American Indian Games

Lacrosse is an old sport. The first record of it comes from the 1600s. It might be even older. It began as a game American Indians played for centuries. Many tribes across North America played it, including the Iroquois, Cherokees, and Ojibwa. It was especially popular in the northeastern part of North America.

American Indians played many sports. Some games used sticks to push a ball along the ground. But one game was different. It used sticks with nets so players could pick up, catch, and throw the ball.

This early version of lacrosse was a major cultural event. The fields were huge—sometimes miles long. Players numbered in the hundreds or thousands. The game was fun, but it was also good training for war.

Centuries ago, American Indians played a game like lacrosse.

1636

Year of the first written record describing lacrosse, by French missionary Jean de Brébeuf.

- Native people played lacrosse for centuries.
- The game differed from other early sports through use of a netted stick.
- Early versions of the game involved huge fields and sometimes thousands of players.
- Colonial Europeans modified the rules to create the modern game.

LA CROSSE

Different American Indian tribes had their own names for lacrosse in their native languages. Many names meant "to hit." When French settlers saw the game, they named it *la crosse*, meaning "the stick." Eventually the name became one word: *lacrosse*.

Lacrosse was unlike other native sports because of the netted stick.

Colonial Europeans discovered the game after entering the New World. They made the field smaller and added their own rules. But today's lacrosse is basically the same as its early version. Players pass the ball, catch it, and shoot it into a goal. That simple beauty is one of the reasons people love lacrosse.

Lacrosse Is One Sport but Two Games

One of the best features of lacrosse is that it's two games in one. There are two versions of lacrosse: box lacrosse and field lacrosse. Box lacrosse is played indoors on a covered hockey rink. Field lacrosse is played outdoors on a field about the size of a football field.

Box lacrosse is the faster version. There are six players per team. It almost resembles basketball. There is a 30-second shot clock for the team with the ball to take their shot.

Box lacrosse is played in a hockey rink without ice.

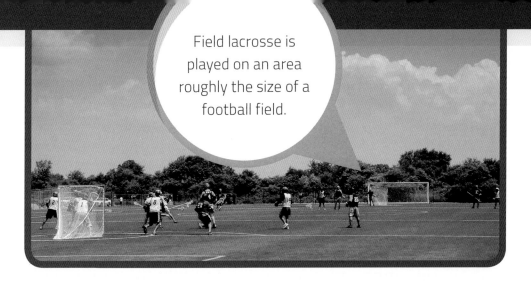

Field lacrosse is played on an area roughly the size of a football field.

Because field lacrosse is played on a larger area, the game is more open. Passes are longer. There also is no shot clock. Teams can possess the ball as long as they are able. There are 10 players per side.

Box lacrosse was created in Canada. Canadians enjoy field lacrosse, too, but the cold winters make it hard to play outdoor lacrosse year-round. So Canadians developed the indoor version of the game. Of the two, box lacrosse is now more popular in Canada.

1931
Year the first indoor lacrosse game was held in Montreal, Canada.

- Lacrosse has two versions: box and field lacrosse.
- Box lacrosse is played indoors, field lacrosse is played outdoors.
- Box lacrosse has a smaller field and fewer players.
- Field lacrosse is played on a large field with more players.

WOMEN'S LACROSSE

The general object of lacrosse is the same for men and women. But women's lacrosse has a few different rules. The field is slightly larger, and there are more players. Body contact is not allowed in women's lacrosse. Women players only need to wear eye protection and mouthguards. They don't need to wear full helmets as the men do.

Lacrosse Grows in Popularity

There's no question: lacrosse is booming. More and more people play lacrosse each year. This is true at the youth, high school, and college levels. In the United States, the number of lacrosse players grew more than 300 percent between 2001 and 2015.

The reasons for the boom are pretty simple. Lacrosse is easy to learn. It doesn't require much equipment. It's fast and exciting to watch and play.

Plus, lacrosse isn't as risky as some other sports. Lacrosse is a contact sport. That means players

High school lacrosse is a quickly growing sport.

THINK ABOUT IT

What sports or activities do you participate in? Why did you decide to try that activity? What would you say to a friend to convince him or her to try it?

400,000

Number of youth players in the United States in 2015.

- Lacrosse is one of the world's fastest-growing sports.
- More high schools and colleges add it every year.
- Lacrosse is growing faster than any other high school sport.
- Countries around the world now play lacrosse as well.

sometimes collide during play. But lacrosse doesn't have as much contact as do hockey or football. There are fewer injury risks.

Thousands of high school students now play the sport. From 2010 to 2015, the number of high schools playing lacrosse increased by nearly 30 percent. It is also the fastest-growing college sport.

Lacrosse was once only popular in Canada and the northeastern United States. That's where the sport first began. But lacrosse is now spreading to the rest of North America. It's also spreading even farther. It's now played on every continent except Antarctica. People all across the world are beginning to enjoy lacrosse.

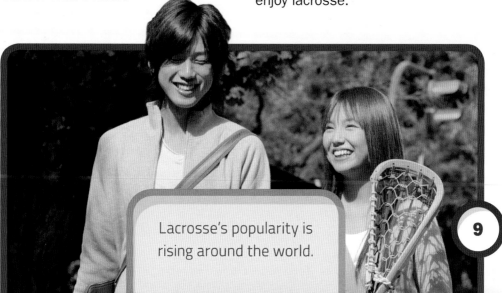

Lacrosse's popularity is rising around the world.

9

Pro Lacrosse Is the Game's Biggest Stage

There are two major professional men's lacrosse leagues in the world. Major League Lacrosse (MLL) is a field lacrosse league. The teams play in the United States. The National Lacrosse League (NLL) plays a form of box lacrosse. The teams are from the United States and Canada.

The MLL began play in 2001. It's played outdoors. Its season lasts from April to August. Nine teams make up the league. Paul Rabil and Kieran McArdle are some of the league's best scorers.

The NLL was first known as the Eagle Pro Box Lacrosse League.

The MLL has great players, such as Kieran McArdle.

Then it became the Major Indoor Lacrosse League. It finally became the NLL after the 1997 season. The NLL has nine teams in the United States and Canada. The NLL season runs from January to April. Shawn Evans and Dhane Smith are some of the top players.

Shawn Evans is an NLL star player.

For many years, there was no women's professional lacrosse league. That changed in 2016 with the creation of the United Women's Lacrosse League. Four teams took the field in the first season.

DON'T QUIT YOUR DAY JOB

Many professional athletes make millions of dollars. But most players in the MLL make between $10,000 and $20,000. For that reason, a lot of players have full-time jobs outside the sport. Brett Schmidt plays for the Charlotte Hounds on the weekends. But he works in finance during the week.

245,528
Total attendance for all games in the 2015 MLL season.

- Lacrosse has two major men's professional leagues: the MLL and the NLL.
- The MLL is a field lacrosse league.
- The NLL plays a form of box lacrosse.
- The first women's lacrosse league began play in 2016.

11

Lacrosse Is Canada's National Summer Sport

Fast players. Rocket-fast shots. Lots of goals. Lacrosse is very similar to hockey. It's no wonder Canadians are crazy for both sports. In 1994, hockey was named Canada's national winter sport. Lacrosse was named its national summer sport.

Canadians enjoy both box lacrosse and field lacrosse. Of the two, box lacrosse is more popular in the country. Canadians created box lacrosse.

Many of the best box lacrosse players are Canadian. All but one player on the 2016 NLL champion Saskatchewan Rush were from Canada. Also, the Canadian men's and women's national teams are regularly ranked first or second in the world. Canada has many youth

Team Canada often leads the world in lacrosse.

leagues as well. This means Canada will likely remain one of the world's best teams for generations to come.

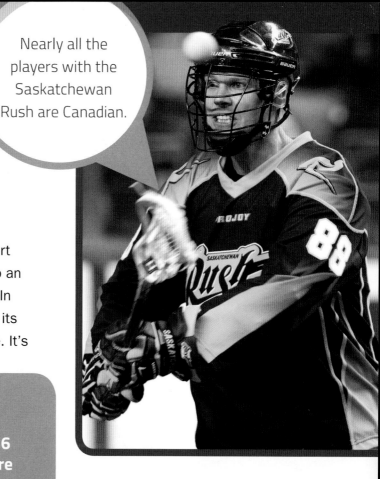

Nearly all the players with the Saskatchewan Rush are Canadian.

Lacrosse is an important part of Canada's history. It's also an important part of its future. In 2017, Canada will celebrate its 150th year of independence. It's

90

Percentage of 2016 NLL players who are Canadian.

- In 1994, lacrosse was designated Canada's national summer sport.
- Box lacrosse was invented in Canada and has been popular there ever since.
- Most pro lacrosse players are from Canada, and the country's national teams are among the best in the world.
- The Canadian Lacrosse Association will celebrate its 150th anniversary in 2017.

also the 150th anniversary of the Canadian Lacrosse Association. The organization has overseen lacrosse in Canada since 1867. It was first called the National Lacrosse Association. The anniversary celebration will honor lacrosse history. Native Canadian artists will craft handmade lacrosse sticks. And of course, there will be lacrosse games and tournaments. Some games will include rules from old forms of the sport.

6

Lacrosse Spreads around the World

For most of its history, lacrosse has been popular only in North America. But that's changing as more people across the globe learn about the game.

The Federation of International Lacrosse (FIL) has members in more than 50 countries. Teams compete in international tournaments. Men's teams play for the FIL World Championship every four years. Women play in the Women's World Cup every four years as well.

The first FIL World Championship was held in 1967. As of 2016, the US team has won all but three cups. Canada has won the others. The United States has been dominant in the Women's World Cup as well. A women's championship has been played every four years since 1982.

55

Number of nations that belong to the FIL as of 2016.

- Lacrosse is growing in popularity around the world.
- The FIL hosts international lacrosse championship tournaments.
- The FIL aims to make lacrosse an Olympic sport by 2024.

THE IROQUOIS NATIONALS

One of the sport's best teams is the Iroquois Nationals. The Iroquois were one of the original inventors of lacrosse. The Nationals are the only American Indian team to play an international sport as a member nation. American Indians from other tribes may play for the Nationals as well.

At the 2014 FIL World Championship, a record 38 teams participated. That number included new teams from places such as Uganda, Israel, and Colombia.

Lacrosse fans hope to see the game in the Olympics. The sport was officially included in the Olympics in 1904 and 1908. It has been a demonstration sport three other times. That means it was played, but no medals were awarded. The FIL hopes to return lacrosse to the Olympics in 2024.

Australia and the United States compete in the FIL Women's World Cup.

Lacrosse Legends Are in Halls of Fame

Most sports have halls of fame that honor their greatest athletes. Lacrosse has two major halls of fame.

The National Lacrosse Hall of Fame is in Baltimore, Maryland. Since 1957, the hall has inducted players and other important people in United States lacrosse. More than 400 people have been inducted as of 2016. The hall also features a museum.

The Canadian Lacrosse Hall of Fame is located in New Westminster, British Columbia. It has more than 500 inductees as of 2016. The hall celebrates players as well as people

The National Lacrosse Hall of Fame features photos and equipment from the sport's past.

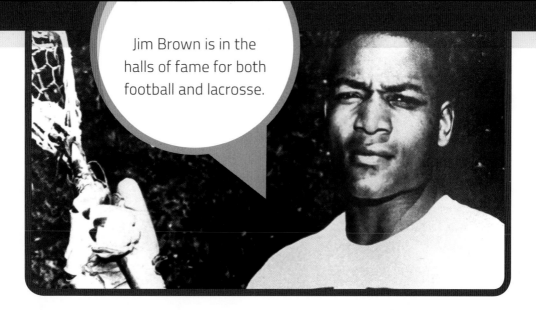

Jim Brown is in the halls of fame for both football and lacrosse.

who helped grow the game. The hall even includes the entire Canadian national team that won the 1928 Olympics, when lacrosse was a demonstration event.

Perhaps the most famous name in a lacrosse hall of fame is Jim Brown. Brown was a star running back in the National Football League. He also played lacrosse at Syracuse University. One year, he was second in the nation with 43 goals. He is in the Pro Football Hall of Fame and the National Lacrosse Hall of Fame.

9
Number of new members inducted to each hall of fame in 2016.

- Lacrosse has two major halls of fame. One is in the United States, and one is in Canada.
- The National Lacrosse Hall of Fame has more than 400 inductees.
- The Canadian Lacrosse Hall of Fame has more than 500 inductees.
- Jim Brown is in both the Pro Football Hall of Fame and the National Lacrosse Hall of Fame.

THINK ABOUT IT

Jim Brown was a star in both lacrosse and football in college. What would it be like to be great in two sports? What traits and skills would you need for both sports?

Collegiate Lacrosse Expands for Both Genders

Sports are very popular on campus. Lacrosse is the fastest-growing college sport in the United States. Dozens of schools have added lacrosse teams. From 2001 to 2014, the number of players grew by 95 percent for men and by 109 percent for women.

In 2016, a record 178 schools played Division I lacrosse. There were 68 men's teams and 110 women's teams. Across all the college divisions, there are more than 30,000 lacrosse players.

The top college men's and women's teams compete each year for a national championship. Sixteen teams qualify for each tournament. For years, the best college teams were in New England. That's where the sport has always been popular. But that's changing as the sport

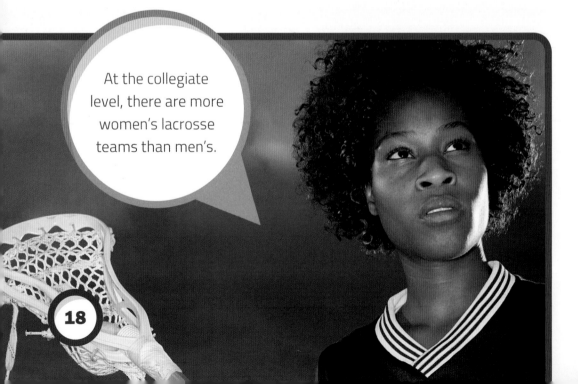

At the collegiate level, there are more women's lacrosse teams than men's.

11

Number of schools that have won the men's college lacrosse championship in the 45 years between 1971 and 2016.

- Lacrosse is the fastest-growing college sport in the United States.
- A total of 178 men's and women's teams played college lacrosse in 2016.
- Schools play in tournaments to name a national champion.
- Some college lacrosse rivalries go back to the 1800s.

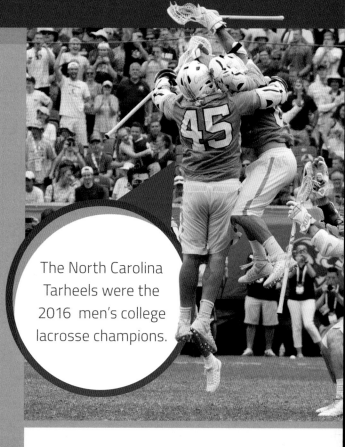

The North Carolina Tarheels were the 2016 men's college lacrosse champions.

grows. North Carolina won both the men's and women's tournaments in 2016.

In all college sports, fans enjoy rivalries between schools. Some college lacrosse rivalries go back many years. Cornell University and Hobart College have played each other since 1896. Other lacrosse rivalries are newer but just as intense. Some rivalries involve not just two but three schools.

A NEW LACROSSE HOTBED

The year 2015 was big in the history of college lacrosse. The University of Denver won the men's national championship. It was the first school from outside the Eastern time zone ever to win the men's tournament.

19

Practice Makes Perfect in Lacrosse

All athletes work hard to get better at their game. Lacrosse players also need to practice to become the best. Practice sessions build the skills and muscles needed to play the game.

Wall ball is one of the most important drills in lacrosse practice. A player stands a few feet from a wall. The player tosses a ball against the wall, then catches it. This is repeated over and over. Experts recommend 30 minutes of wall ball each day. It will help players feel more comfortable with passing and catching.

There's a lot of running in a lacrosse game. Calisthenics, a type of exercise, can help players run longer.

Good warmups and stretching also get the body ready to run.

Lacrosse players must be light and quick on their feet. Running around cones can help develop good footwork. In another helpful

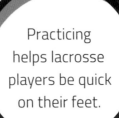

Practicing helps lacrosse players be quick on their feet.

Lacrosse players spend a lot of time on drills that improve passing and catching.

drill, players lay their sticks in front of them horizontally. They step over the sticks with one foot, then the other. Then they step back with the first foot. They repeat the steps back and forth.

In men's lacrosse, body contact is allowed. Players often collide and bump. That's why players need to be strong. They need to push other players away. Working with medicine balls helps strengthen the upper body. Weight training also builds arm strength for male and female players.

5
Number of miles (8 km) a lacrosse player can run during a game.

- Practice and exercise help lacrosse players become great.
- Drills such as wall ball help players with passing and catching.
- Running drills help players build enough energy to last a whole game.
- Weight training can build strength needed in contact games.

Lacrosse Is the Fastest Game on Foot

Lacrosse is sometimes called the fastest sport on two feet. It has super-fast shots and sprinting players.

Most lacrosse shots are between 80 and 100 miles per hour (129 to 161 km/h). At those speeds, goalies have only a fraction of a second to react. The fastest lacrosse shot on record traveled 119.9 miles per hour (192.9 km/h). Patrick Luehrsen of Libertyville, Illinois, hit that speed in 2015. He did it with a special stick he made himself.

The key to high-speed shots is in the whipping action. Players bring the stick back and swing it around their

Fast players and fast shots make lacrosse exciting.

0.25

Seconds a goalie has to react to an 80-mile-per-hour (128.7-km/h) shot from 30 feet (9.1 m) away.

- Lacrosse is known as the fastest sport on two feet.
- Patrick Luehrsen has the all-time fastest lacrosse shot of 119.9 miles per hour (192.9 km/h).
- The rotation of a player's body is key to a fast shot.
- Lacrosse fan Zach Dorn set the MLL record at the 2014 All-Star Skills Competition.

an MLL record of 113 miles per hour (182 km/h). He did that at the 2013 MLL All-Star Skills Competition. However, that record was broken the very next year—by fan Zach Dorn. Dorn was a former high school lacrosse player. He won a chance to participate in the fastest-shot event with the MLL players.

bodies. This generates a lot of power.

Another key to fast shots is how fast the player is running. When running, a player creates energy. That energy then goes into the shot. It gives it an extra boost.

So far, no player has beaten Luehrsen's record speed. But some can get close. Mike Sawyer of the Charlotte Hounds set

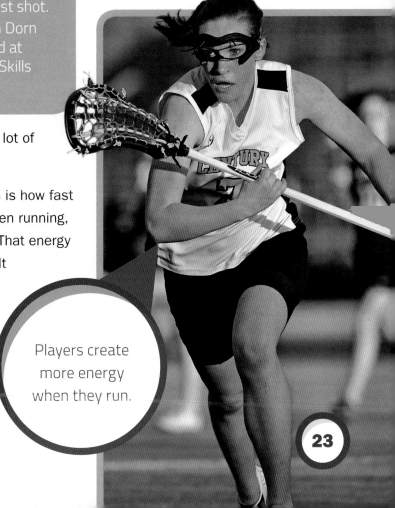

Players create more energy when they run.

Lacrosse Offers Fun and Health Benefits

Lacrosse is certainly an exciting sport to play. But it's also a fun way to get a great workout. Lacrosse players enjoy many health benefits. They see the effects in their bodies and minds.

Lacrosse players often run several miles per game. It's a high-impact workout. All that running burns calories. It's good for the heart and lungs, too. With every run, those organs get stronger. Having a stronger heart and lungs helps lacrosse players run longer and perform better. That's good on and off the field.

Lacrosse works other parts of the body, too. Swinging the stick builds arm muscles. Cradling the ball builds wrist strength. Also, lacrosse

Running in lacrosse makes the heart and lungs stronger.

60

Minutes of fun and fitness in a regulation lacrosse game.

- Playing lacrosse has many health benefits.
- Lacrosse involves a lot of running that strengthens the heart and lungs.
- Lacrosse works many different muscles.
- Players also see brain benefits.

helps build hand-eye coordination. To play well, players must use their hands and eyes together. It's another way lacrosse helps the body perform better.

Lacrosse is not just a physical activity, however. There's also a mental part of the game. Players must decide when to pass and when to shoot. The more often players make these types of decisions, the better they get at them. Playing lacrosse helps the brain in other ways as well. It releases chemicals that help relieve stress and improve mood.

> Many players love lacrosse simply because it's fun.

All these health benefits are great reasons to play lacrosse. But most people play for one main reason: it's fun. Lacrosse is a simple sport, but it's hard to master. That challenge keeps players coming back for more.

Lacrosse Has Its Own Slang and Culture

For players, lacrosse is more than just a sport. It's a culture and lifestyle. Lacrosse players live their sport on and off the field. Many players grow up enjoying the sport from a young age. By the time they're adults, lacrosse has been a major part of their lives for years.

Lacrosse even has its own language. Players usually call the game "lax." Players are "laxers." Good laxers are "ballers." Some bad ones are called "fish." A stick is a "crosse." A ball is a "bullet." The goal is the "cage." A player who doesn't stretch out to catch a pass has

Lacrosse players call their sport "lax."

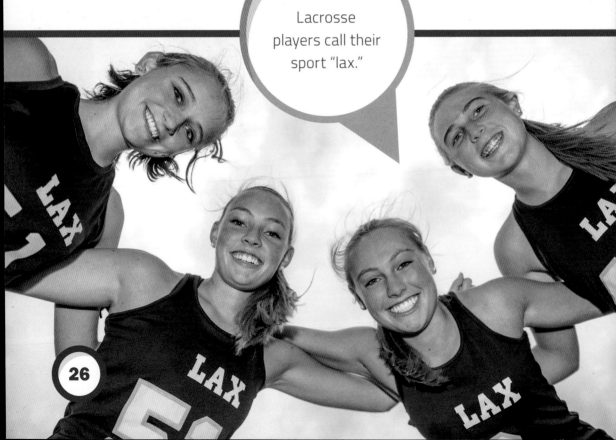

8.5

Average age youth players first begin playing lacrosse.

- Lacrosse players have a unique culture and language.
- There are many slang terms in lacrosse.
- Some original forms of the sport are still played today.
- Several celebrities are part of the lacrosse culture.

THINK ABOUT IT

Can you think of other sports that have special slang terms? Why do sports players develop their own slang and cultures?

"alligator arms." The list of slang terms goes on and on.

Today's lacrosse culture honors its history. Some native versions of lacrosse are still played centuries later. Toli is a Choctaw version of lacrosse. Stickball is a Cherokee form.

Lacrosse players are devoted to their sport. Some carry their sticks with them everywhere they go. This is especially true in the Northeast, where many players grow up with the sport.

Several celebrities played lacrosse when they were growing up. Musician Dave Grohl of the Foo Fighters grew up in Virginia. He played goalie before choosing music full time. Actor Steve Carell played lacrosse in high school in Massachusetts.

Dave Grohl, lead singer of the Foo Fighters, played lacrosse.

27

Fact Sheet

- Nobody knows exactly how old lacrosse is. It dates back many centuries for American Indians. The first records of it come from European explorers in the 1600s. That makes it hard to know where and when lacrosse started. The net on the stick makes lacrosse different from other stick-and-ball games. Evidence of lacrosse has been found only in eastern North America.

- The first men's college lacrosse championship was played in 1971. The first women's championship was held in 1982. Syracuse University has the most titles in men's lacrosse (10), while the University of Maryland has the most in the women's game (12). Maryland won seven straight women's championships from 1995 to 2001.

- A version of lacrosse without body contact is called intercrosse. The basket of the stick is all plastic, and the ball is hollow. This makes it suitable for indoor play. It is often played in schools for physical education classes.

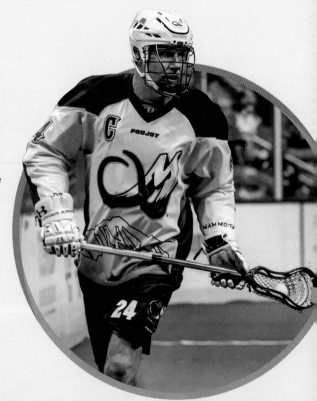

Goalies in lacrosse have a huge basket on their stick to stop the ball. But this makes it hard to pass the ball to teammates. Goalies typically stay close to the net, but they may run out if they want. Goalie Brett Queener of Albany College scored five goals in his college career, a record for goalies.

Glossary

calisthenics
Exercises that involve no special equipment or devices.

campus
The grounds of a college or university.

contact
In sports, when players collide or come together during gameplay.

drill
A physical or mental exercise that builds skill through regular practice.

hand-eye coordination
Using visual information to help guide the hand to complete a task, such as catching a ball.

league
A collection of teams that compete against one another.

rivalry
A fierce and ongoing competition between two or more teams.

settler
A person who establishes a new city or territory.

slang
Informal terms used by a particular group of people.

tournament
A competition where teams who lose get knocked out.

For More Information

Books

Bowker, Paul D. *Total Lacrosse*. Minneapolis, MN: Abdo, 2017.

Jones, Cameron and Chris Hayhurst. *An Insider's Guide to Lacrosse*. New York: Rosen, 2015.

Tometich, Annabelle. *Lacrosse*. Minneapolis, MN: Abdo, 2012.

Visit 12StoryLibrary.com

Scan the code or use your school's login at **12StoryLibrary.com** for recent updates about this topic and a full digital version of this book. Enjoy free access to:

- Digital ebook
- Breaking news updates
- Live content feeds
- Videos, interactive maps, and graphics
- Additional web resources

Note to educators: Visit 12StoryLibrary.com/register to sign up for free premium website access. Enjoy live content plus a full digital version of every 12-Story Library book you own for every student at your school.

Index

About the Author

Todd Kortemeier is a journalist and children's author from Minnesota. He has written more than 50 books for young people, primarily on sports topics. He and his wife live in Minneapolis.